CHAPTER ONE

THE BASIC IDEA; THINKING ABOUT COMICS

Y'know, it's a funny old world. Last year Mad Dog referred to me as the Che Guevara of the comic industry. Last week, Dave Gibbons informed me that I was now its Terry Wogan. Although I have no idea how this startling metamorphosis came about, I must reluctantly accept it as the unadorned truth and wait in terror for the final, inevitable transformation into Pete Murray. Even with that said, however, I'm afraid I find my tendencies towards self-publicity almost impossible to restrain, so stand prepared as the most overexposed man in funnybooks whips it out once again.

The biggest difficulty in writing about any creative activity, from writing itself to automobile-devouring, is that in most cases the articles or interviews that result seem to be unable to rise above plain technical information and lists of preferred tools. I don't want to fall into the same rut here by telling you which typewriter I use or what sort of carbon paper · I think is best, since this information will not make the slightest difference to how well you write. Similarly, I don't think that a precise breakdown of my work process would be of much use, since I find it tends to vary wildly from story to story and that all writers tend to develop their own approach in response to their own circumstances.

Above all, I don't want to produce anything that smacks even remotely of "How to Write Comics the Alan Moore Way." Teaching a generation of emergent artists or writers how to copy the generation that came before was a stupid idea when Marvel introduced their "How to Draw..." book and it would be equally irresponsible of me to instruct up-and-coming writers on how to write sickly extravagant captions like "Dawn transformed the sky into an abattoir" or whatever. John Buscema is a fine artist, but the industry doesn't need 50 people who draw like him any more than it needs people who write like me.

Bearing all of the above in mind, what I'd like to attempt is something that tackles the broader issue of how we might actually **think** about the craft of comic writing, rather than a list of detailed specifics. I'd like to talk about the approaches and thought processes that underlie writing as a whole rather than about the way those processes are finally put down upon paper. As I see the situation, the way we think about the act of writing will inevitably shape the works that we produce. Judging from most of the current output of the major comic companies, it seems to me that a large contributing factor to their general lifelessness must be the stagnant thought processes from which they sprang. Certainly, in terms of the general standard of writing in comics at the moment I tend to see the same mechanical plot structures and the same functional approach to characterization being used over and over again, to the point where people find it increasingly difficult to imagine that there could ever be a different way of doing things. As our basic assumptions about our craft become increasingly outmoded, we find that it becomes more of a problem to create work with any relevance to the rapidly altering world in which the industry and the readers that support it actually exist. By "relevance," incidentally, I don't just mean stories about race relations and pollution, although that's certainly a big part of it. I mean stories that actually have some sort of meaning in relation to the world about us, stories that reflect the nature and the texture of life in the

closing years of the 20th century. Stories that are **useful** in some way. Admittedly, it would be fairly easy for the industry to survive comfortably for a while by pandering to specialist-group nostalgia or simple escapism, but the industry that concerns itself entirely with areas of this sort is in my view impotent and worthy of little more consideration or interest than the greeting card industry.

Whether for better or worse, society as we understand it will be going through some almost incomprehensible changes during the next 40 years. Assuming that the changes are survivable (and there seems little point in assuming anything else), and assuming that we have a future, then we are eventually going to have to cope with it. The choice to me seems fairly straightforward: Either we ride the wave of change or we're borne away by it. This applies to the world in general, but obviously, for our purposes here we're applying it specifically to the area that we, as professional and non-professional comic enthusiasts, have some degree of control over. If comics are to survive, they need both to change and to become flexible enough to withstand a process of almost **continual** change thereafter. Changing the trappings of the comic industry isn't enough. New printing techniques, new characters, new computer graphic facilities...none of these will make the slightest scrap of difference unless the fundamental assumptions upon which the artform itself rests are challenged and modified to fit times for which they were not originally designed. You can produce a comic about bright and interesting new characters, have a computer draw it, publish it in a lavish Baxter package and color it with the most sophisticated laser scan techniques available, and the chances are that it will still be tepid, barely readable shit.

The reason why comic writing is perhaps even a greater cause for concern than comic book drawing is that writing comes at the very start of the process. If the thinking behind the writing is inadequate, the script is inadequate. Consequently, even in the hands of the best artist in the world, the finished comic will lack something that no amount of flashy coloring or printing can hope to compensate for. To change comics, we must change the way we think about their creation, and the following exploration should be seen as only the first few clumsy steps that end.

For want of anywhere better to begin, perhaps it might be interesting to start with a broad consideration of comics and their possibilities and work our way inwards from there. In order to think about comics you have to have some idea of the identity of the thing under consideration. This is where we run into our first difficulty: in attempting to define comics, most commentators have ventured little further than drawing comparisons between the medium and other, more widely acceptable, artforms. Comics are spoken in terms of the cinema, and indeed most of the working vocabulary that I use every day in panel directions to whichever artist I happen to be working with is derived entirely from the cinema. I talk in terms of close-ups, long shots, zooms and pans. It's a handy means of conveying precise visual instructions,

but it also tends to define comic book values in our mind as being virtually indistinguishable from cinematic values. While cinematic thinking has undoubtedly produced many of the finest comic works of the past 30 years, as a model to base our own medium upon I find it eventually to be limiting and restricting. For one thing, any emulation of film technique by the comics medium must inevitably suffer by the comparison. Sure, you can use cinematic panel progressions to make your work more involving and lively than that of comic artists who **haven't** mastered the trick yet, but in the final analysis you will be left with a film that has neither movement nor a soundtrack. The use of cinematic techniques can advance the standards of comic art and writing, but if those techniques are seen as the highest point to which comic art can aspire, then the medium is condemned forever to be a poor relative of the motion picture industry. That isn't good enough.

Comics are also viewed in literary terms, in an effort to draw comparisons between comic sequences and conventional literary forms. Thus, the comic book "short story" is modelled closely upon the classic formula of writers like O. Henry and Saki, with the surprise payoff in the last panel. More inanely, comic work of more than 40 pages is automatically equated with a novel, once more suffering badly from the comparison. With the best will in the world, if you try to describe the Dazzler graphic novel in the same terms as you describe *Moby Dick* then you're simply asking for trouble. As opposed to films without movement or sound we get novels without scope,

depth or purpose. That isn't good enough, either.

Making matters worse, even in using the techniques of other mediums there is a tendency for creators within the comic medium to stay firmly rooted in the past. Looking at what is described as cinematic work in comics we find that we are usually looking at someone who has taken their idea of cinema almost entirely from the work of Will Eisner, or rather from the work that Eisner was doing 30 or 40 years ago. Not a bad place to start, admittedly, except that most people seem to finish there as well. Eisner, in the heyday of *The Spirit*, utilized the cinematic techniques of people like Orson Welles to brilliant effect. His imitators use the cinematic techniques of Orson Welles also, at second hand, forgetting that Eisner was learning from the culture surrounding him at the time. Cinema

in comics means Welles, Alfred Hitchcock and maybe a couple of others, all of whom did their best work thirty years ago. Why is there no attempt to understand and adapt the work of contemporary pioneers like Nick Roeg or Altman or Coppola, if a true cinematic approach if what we are aiming for? (Actually, I should perhaps point out at this juncture that the estimable Bryan Talbot did a cracking job of utilizing some of Nick Roeg's techniques in his Luther Arkwright epic, but that's the exception which proves the rule.) Why must the literary values of comics be determined by the values of 30- to 40-year-old pulp fiction, whatever the merits of that pulp fiction may be?

Rather than seizing upon the superficial similarities between comics and films or comics and books in the hope that some of the respectability of those media will rub off upon us, wouldn't it be more constructive to focus our attention upon those ideas where comics are special and unique? Rather than dwelling upon film techniques that comics can duplicate, shouldn't we perhaps consider comic techniques that films **can't** duplicate?

As an illustration of the kind of thinking I mean, let's just consider a film that I have not seen but have only heard about second-hand. It's called "The Draftsman's Contract," and most people I know who have seen the thing reacted in exactly the same way. They said that it was an excellent and brilliantly constructed film with some of the most finely written dialogue that they'd come across. They also said that they felt they'd have to see it another two or three times before they fully appreciated it in all its complexity. Random lines of dialogue at the beginning have meaningful echoes and resonance in the light of scenes later in the film, but unless you can remember every incidental remark or piece of conversation you're almost certain to miss a lot of them.

Hearing about this, it struck me that the film must have been written with an eye to construction very much like that used by novelists as opposed to that used by screenwriters. You see, a novel can get away with literary complexity; the reader will absorb the thing at his or her own pace and can refer back to earlier sequences at the turn of a page. In this way the novel can be appreciated to the full extent and can achieve that degree of depth and resonance found in a lot of good novels but very few comic books or films. While theoretically I could have read *Gravity's Rainbow* by Thomas Pynchon in a little under eight hours at my current reading speed, I chose to take two months and read the thing properly, making sure that I missed as little as possible. In a cinema, I wouldn't be able to make that choice. Whereas a novelization of "The Draftsman's Contract" might take me six weeks to ingest, if I'm watching a film I'm trapped in the rigid framework dictated by the film's running time. I must immerse myself in the flow of the film and hope I'll pick up on enough of the constant flow of details to make coherent sense of the story at the end. Even so, there is a limit to just how much the human mind can absorb and make sense of in a strictly defined period of time. In terms of effect upon the reader or viewer, this gives films a limitation

that books do not necessarily have to suffer from.

Of course, it isn't entirely one-sided. There are a lot of things that can be done with a film that can't be done with a short story or novel. Information can be presented visually in an efficient and measured fashion concerning character and environment that would take a lot of bulky description and exposition to convey with words alone. Also, since our current society has a greater visual orientation than a literary one, a visual flow of narrative gives a much more immediate and involving sensory impact to the work in hand, even though much of the emotional depth and resonance is forfeit in many cases.

The point of all this muddled rambling is that it occurred to me that a comic strip version of "The Draftsman's Contract" would have in many ways the best of both worlds. Given sufficient intelligence on the part of the creators involved there's no reason why the comic-strip work shouldn't have all the depth and complexity of the book, and the visual flow and appeal of the film, and at the same time be read and appreciated at whatever pace the reader finds most appropriate. In terms of intellectual and emotional effect upon the reader, this seems to represent an edge that comics would do well to exploit. In the end, it is **effect** which governs the success of an individual piece of artwork or a whole artform, and while abstract critical considerations concerning the inherent quality of a work might give us a few useful handles with which to grasp and appreciate a work more fully, art still succeeds or fails in terms of the actual effect it has upon the individual members of its audience. If it stimulates or excites them, they will respond to it. If it doesn't, they'll go and look for something that does. Comics have a capacity for effect that they haven't begun to take advantage of, and are held back by narrow and increasingly obsolete notions of what constitutes a comic story. In order for comics to move forward as a medium, these notions must change.

Whereas once it was believed that the granting of more creative freedom or partial ownership of their work to the artists and writers in the industry would produce a surge of breathtaking creativity and invention, this turns out not to be the case. With a very few bold exceptions, most of the creator-owned material produced by the Independent companies has been almost indistinguishable from the mainstream product that preceded it. It seems to me that this demonstrates that the problem is not primarily one of working conditions or incentive; the problem is creative, and it's on a basic creative level that it must be solved. I don't think that this solution will come about without a drastic improvement in the standard of comic writing, since, as I pointed out earlier, the writer is at the beginning of the whole creative process. To this end, then, we'll move on and I'll try my best to outline some of the problems and the potential that I see in various aspects of comic writing. Obviously, most of these observations are drawn from my own experience and thus must be regarded as highly subjective: There are no doubt better ways to handle all of the different elements that I'll be examining below, but this is the way that I personally try to tackle them, for what that's worth. I'm more concerned with presenting an idea of the level of thinking that is appropriate for comics than with suggesting that I've devised any concrete answers, but hopefully the ideas and techniques mentioned hereunder might provide a jumping-off point from which those who are interested can progress toward their own conclusions and solutions.

Once more, the difficulty is in knowing where to start. The range of considerations that must be brought to bear upon even the simplest comic story is extensive, and it doesn't really matter which component we choose to examine first. All of them are connected, and all of them have bearing on each other. Thus, we may as well get the more intangible and abstract elements out of the way first before progressing to the finer and more precise aspects of the craft. A good starting point would perhaps be the aspect that lies at the very heart of any creative process: the idea.

The idea is what the story is about; not the plot of the story, or the unfolding of events within that story, but what the story is essentially **about.** As an example from my own work (not because it's a particularly good example but because I can speak with more authority about it than I can about the work of other people) I would cite issue #40 of *Swamp Thing*, "The Curse." This story was **about** the difficulties endured by women in masculine societies, using the common taboo of menstruation as the central motif. This was **not** the plot of the story—the **plot** concerned a young married woman moving into a new home built upon the site of an old Indian lodge and finding herself possessed by the dominating spirit that still resided there, turning her into a form of werewolf. I hope the distinction here is clear between idea and plot, because it's an important one and one ignored by too many writers. Most comic book stories have plots in which the sole concern is the struggle between two or more antagonists. The resolution of the struggle, usually involving some deus ex machina display of a superpower, is the resolution of the plot as well. Beyond the most vague and pointless banality like "Good will always triumph over evil" there is no real central idea in the majority of comics, other than the idea of conflict as interesting in itself.

Naturally, the idea needn't always be a deep, meaningful and significant one. There are lots of different kinds of ideas, ranging from the "What if...?" ideas that lie behind most science-fiction writing to the idea of everyday life as an object of worth and fascination, as seen in the work of Harvey Pekar or Eddie Campbell. "What if..." ideas are the basis for most short science-fiction stories of the "future shock" variety, examples from my own work being short five-page items like 'The Reversible Man" (What if people perceived time as running the opposite way?), "A Place in the Sun" (What if it were possible for human beings to live on the sun?), or "Grawks Bearing Gifts" (What if a group of coarse and vulgar aliens did to our society what our society did to the Red Indians and other aboriginal tribes?). The nature of the idea isn't really important, what is important is simply that there **is** an idea in there somewhere. It can be silly and frivolous, perhaps just a single gag idea, or it can be complex and profound. The only thing that the idea

should definitely be is interesting on some level or another—whether as a brief entertainment designed to hold the attention for five minutes or a lengthier and more thoughtful work intended to engage the mind long after the comic has been put down.

Where ideas actually originate from is seemingly a major preoccupation for most people interested in learning how to write comics and is probably the single question that creative people get asked most often. Unsurprisingly, it's also the question that most often goes unanswered. If forced by threat of torture to give a concise answer, I'd probably say that ideas seem to germinate at a point of cross-fertilization between one's artistic influences and one's own experience. Studying the work of other people will provide useful pointers as to how to formulate an idea, but the initial raw impetus comes from inside the writer or creator themselves, influenced by their opinions, their prejudices, by all the things that have happened to them and by all the elements in their lives that go toward making them the sort of person that they are. There is no substitute for practical experience, and if you want to write about people you ought to put down that comic book and go out and meet some of them rather than studying the way that Stan Lee or Chris Claremont depict people.

It becomes a matter of tuning your perceptions to notice little quirks of circumstance that might otherwise slip by unnoticed, studying your own behavior and the behavior of people and events surrounding you, until you feel you have developed a coherent angle upon life and reality, at least one which relates to a perspective upon events that will suggest original and individual story ideas. Eddie Campbell, to refer again to an example given earlier, has developed an extraordinarily quirky and perceptive eye for the trivia of existence, and it is this that allows him to transform things which might otherwise have seemed ordinary and unremarkable into something at once revealing and entertaining. My point is that you can't teach people to have insights and ideas like Eddie does...you just have to get your head pointing a certain way in regard to how you view life, and you'll find that the ideas then occur spontaneously with hardly any prompting at all. A unique and new viewpoint is never short of unique and new things to say or to talk about. Seen in the right way, everything becomes a source of ideas. Open the paper at the financial page

and read about the escalating international debt crisis, something which may seem incredibly dry and dull on the surface but is actually an exquisitely mad situation that will most probably violently affect the lives of everyone living on this planet over the next few decades. Is there a way that it could be made interesting, perhaps amusing or perhaps frightening, to the average reader? What if you told it in terms of a fantastic allegory, set on an alien planet with something absurd like rat skins instead of money? Would the idea of a bunch of imbecilic aliens irrevocably fouling up their planet over a bunch of rat skins perhaps be amusing? Or how about making it a deadly serious and realistic story by replacing the large national interests involved with individual people, so that the problem can be seen in small, individual human terms, maybe with a loan company operative trying to collect payments in a wild and inhospitable council estate? Is there something there that would hold people's interest for 10 or 15 minutes?

Alternatively, perhaps some incident from your own past will provide the germ of an idea. As a child, for instance, if my parents caught me out in some minor crime that I was convinced they could not possibly know about, it would sometimes occur to me that perhaps adults had some special power of knowing everything, that they kept hidden from children. Indeed, sometimes it seemed that perhaps everybody in the entire world had this ability except me, and that I was the only person excluded from this massive telepathic conspiracy. (If you carry on thinking that sort of stuff beyond the age of nine you're either a paranoid schizophrenic or a comic writer, assuming you care to make a distinction.) Using this irrational childhood fear as a jumping-off point, would it be possible to come up with perhaps a sort of Ray Bradburyesque fantasy about the world of children, or maybe a grim psychological horror story about paranoia as a phenomenon in itself, possibly having the child who suffers the delusions of persecution growing up into a seedy intelligence agent working incognito on the wrong side of the Berlin Wall, in a world where all his childhood terrors have become tangible and real? Please bear in mind that the ideas above are not necessarily meant to be **good** ones...they're just quick off-the-cuff examples of ways in which workable story ideas might be arrived at.

I should perhaps point out that in constructing a story, one doesn't always have to **start** with an idea. It's quite possible to be inspired toward a story by having thought of some purely abstract technical device or panel progression or something. At some point in the process, however, a coherent idea must begin to emerge from the work beyond the simple stylishness of its internal devices. If you happen to think of a neat little four-panel sequence first, that's fine, but you must then try and work out what type of mood or what type of idea the four panels would best express. As an example of this from my own stuff, the original ideas that eventually built up into my first four or five issues of *Swamp Thing* began life as a handful of disconnected ideas for sequences that individually had little meaning. One idea was that it

would be nice to make something of Swamp Thing's capacity for camouflage...maybe have part of his leg or his body visible in the foreground of a panel somewhere with the reader and the other characters in the scene not realizing that they're looking at the swamp creature for a couple of seconds. This eventually became the first two pages of issue #22, "Swamped." An idea I had at the same time involved a way to work the carefully spaced and rhyming Burma Shave billboards that used to run along the freeways of America into a sequence of rhyming captions so that the last line of the rhyme, "...Burma Shave," was on an actual billboard visible in the panel rather than in the caption boxes. This eventually became the last two pages of issue #26, even though I had no idea when I thought of the sequence of what shape it would eventually take or what part it would play in the overall storyline. I kept the idea in abeyance until I had a slot where I could use it, and then when I needed something drastic to happen to the Matt Cable character I hauled it out and turned it into a car-crash scene. The point is that I had to keep the sequences in cold storage until I had a story idea that they would complement. As I said, one doesn't have to start out with an idea, but somewhere along the line a real idea is necessary, assuming the work is to have any impact at all.

CHAPTER TWO

REACHING THE READER; STRUCTURE, PACING, STORY TELLING

We'll assume after last issue that we now have a working idea, something that we wish to say and feel that we can say with conviction. Before we address the problem of exactly how we should go about communicating the idea we should realize that in any act of communication there are at least two participants. In creative terms, these participants are the artist and his or her audience. If you're going to spend a lot of time preparing a communication, it would perhaps be an advantage to at least spend a little considering the person to whom it is addressed.

Obviously, since we are talking about a mass audience of thousands of individual people, there is no way that the artist can understand the likes and dislikes of every single one of them. The conventional response to this problem, at least as evidenced by the behavior of a lot of the major comic companies, is to try to offend no one. I have had at least one editor within the field tell me that there was no point in risking the alienation of even one reader, the solution being to "soften" the dialogue or the scene in question until it had no teeth left with which to maul even the most sensitive member of the audience. Taken to its logical extreme, this suggests that the hypothetical reader that the artist should be aiming his story at is an emotionally overwrought Fauntleroy who faints at the first suggestion of raised voices and bursts into uncomprehending tears at the thought of anything more carnal than a goodnight peck on the forehead. The logic, I suppose, is "Well, at least we haven't offended the most delicate member of our audience, so I guess we haven't offended anybody." This not only reinforces the idea that comics are in some way inherently offensive and will only be tolerated for as long as they keep themselves on a chokingly tight leash, but it also fails to consider for a second the large number of potential readers who don't care to waste their time on innocuous pre-digested pap that reads like literary baby food. There is such a thing as being offensively inoffensive, and while I'm not suggesting for a moment that all comics should be aimed at cynical angst-ridden post-teens, it should be realized that the potential audience out there is far too big and varied to reach by applying **any** restricting criteria based upon a completely unratifiable hypothetical picture of an imaginary "average reader." It would be wrong to see the reader as a whimpering milksop and it would be equally wrong to see the reader as a disaffected streetwise teenager filled with burning proletarian anger against all forms of authority that the writer happens not to agree with. My point is that the whole concept of the "average reader" is completely arse-backwards in that it tries to create a reader that doesn't necessarily exist. I know very few people who would refer to themselves as 'average comic readers', and fewer still who would prove to be truly average if they were put under close examination. Does a medium as small as this one is at present really have a meaningful average that can be drawn from its readership?

In my opinion, the best way to handle the problem is to let the material find its own level and its own audience. If the work has enough central integrity this will almost certainly happen, given time. Admittedly, time is not always a commodity that people can easily afford and I'm sure there are a lot of good works that don't get noticed because of insufficient exposure or because they had to wait too long for an audience to turn up, but even such a harsh system of natural selection and survival of the fittest seems more productive in the long term than hamstringing the work of art at birth in the vain hope of making it puny and unprepossessing enough to avoid the attention of the predators.

But even if we don't base our assumptions about the work we are going to produce upon an imaginary hypothetical reader, it's obvious that we have to find some way to understand the readers' part in the creative process. Once again, I think this becomes less problematic if you tackle the problem from the other end. Instead of thinking about what might possibly affect the reader negatively and then expunging any trace of it from the work, why not think about things likely to affect the reader positively? Again, we have the problem of how to determine what will best affect such a wide spectrum of different people, but at least in this instance there are a couple of useful models to base our thinking upon. One such is the common or garden joke.

Jokes are not generally designed with a specific audience in mind. They just happen. Presumably, somebody somewhere has an amusing thought, works out a way to formulate it to best effect and then tells it to a friend or sells it to a stand-up comedian. From this point the joke spreads out by word of mouth and repetition, affecting thousands of people if only for a few seconds. Strangely, the criteria of what is or is not a good joke don't seem to be so hotly contested as they would be if we

be squeezed out of business or be relegated to working in bottom-of-the-heap sleaze pits where nothing more than vulgarity is demanded. Alternately, if there was some integrity behind all the outrage, the perpetrators become persecuted legends with a fanatical cult following and generally exercise tremendous influence upon the artists that come after them. In comedy, Lenny Bruce is an example. In music, perhaps the Sex Pistols. In comic books, EC would fit the bill.

To get back to our consideration of the reader of comic books whom we are trying to communicate our idea to, let's think about the person who originally comes up with the joke. As noted before, he has no idea of the person who will eventually get to hear his offering...he just thinks that the gag sounds funny. It makes him laugh, so there's a fair chance it will make a lot of other people laugh as well. I dare say that many gag writers and comedians are content to rely upon their intuition as to what is funny, whereas having heard interviews with people like Max Wall it's apparent that many put a great deal of thought into exactly what it is that will make people laugh. There are certain broad principles of humor that are almost certain to arouse a laughter response no matter what the disposition or background of the person hearing the joke might be. Understanding these broad human responses is much more useful as a tool toward creating humor than any consideration of an "average audience member" would be.

were talking about a film or a book or a comic. Some people laugh loudly at it, some people's amusement is a little more restrained, and one or two don't laugh at all. Whatever the reaction, the joke has served its purpose and affected numerous different people to the best of its ability in relation to their individual senses of humor. Sometimes a joke turns up that offends large numbers of people, but nobody ever mounts a campaign to tone down or stamp out jokes in general as a result of this. Sure, if there is one particular comedian who insists on delivering offensive joke after offensive joke then eventually some action might be taken against him or her personally, in which case one of two things happen. If there was no point to being offensive (as with a high number of comedians who frequent the average working men's club) then the perpetrator will either

As a for-instance, in his excellent book *The Act of Creation*, the late Arthur Koestler discussed a number of the broad mechanisms that actually excite humor as a response and a reaction to certain stimuli. He noted that most jokes seem to be based upon building up a set of expectations in the mind of the listener and then totally demolishing all of their assumptions with the unexpected denouement of the punch line. Generally, the punch line of a joke is something that comes as an intellectual surprise to the recipient after he or she has been led to accept the logic of the joke's initial premise. Using the most simple example in the world, "Why did the chicken cross the road?" sets up an expectation in the mind of the listener that the joker wouldn't be asking the question if there were not genuinely some meaningful reason for the bloody chicken to be crossing the bloody road. The punch line, "To get to the other side" (and I'm sorry if I spoiled it for those of you who hadn't yet heard it) completely defeats these expectations by suddenly snapping the question into an unexpected frame of reference. Of **course** it's doing it to get to the other side, but that wasn't the kind of answer that the question led the listener to expect. There is a brief moment of surprise as our brain is tickled by having to switch from one logic system to another without warning, and in response a gland secretes a certain chemical which produces a sort of involuntary muscular and nervous spasm, and we laugh.

By thinking about a basic general process that affects the wide spectrum of human beings rather than whether a specific notion or idea will adversely affect a specific hypothetical reader, it is thus possible to reach an understanding of one of the mechanisms fundamental to human response. Even without a helpful pointer like the Koestler book mentioned above, it's possible to look very closely at one's own reactions and responses and make some helpful deductions about the broad responses of your readership. If you want to write a horror story, first think about what sort of things horrify you. Analyze your own fears thoroughly enough and you might be able to reach some conclusions about the broad mass of human fear and anxiety. Be ruthless about this, and submit yourself to as much emotional pain as is necessary to get the question answered: What horrifies me? Pictures of little kids starving in Africa horrifies me. Why does that horrify me? It horrifies me because I can't stand the thought of tiny children being born into a world of starvation and misery and horror and never knowing anything but hunger and pain and fear, never knowing that there could possibly be anything other than needing food as desperately as a suffocating man needs air, and never hearing anything but weeping and moaning and despair. Yeah, well, okay, but **why** can't I stand that? I can't stand that because I like to perceive the world as having some form of just and fair order, without which much of existence would seem meaningless, and I know that for those children there is no possibility of them perceiving the world in those terms. I also know that were I to be in their situation I wouldn't be able to see any unifying design above the hunger and misery, either. So does that mean that there **is** no order, no point to existence, above all no point to **my** existence? Is that what scares the shit out of me every time I see all those fly-specked bellies on the six o'clock news? Yeah. Yeah, probably it is. What scares me is probably not what's happening to them but what it implies concerning **me**. That isn't a terribly easy noble thing to have to face up to, but it's the sort of wringer that you have to put yourself through in order to have any valuable understanding of the material that you are working with.

The material is human thoughts and human feelings and human ideas. Everything in our world from the family structure to the neutron bomb has its origins within that area, and anybody who intends to mess around in the mass consciousness for a living ought to be aware of the material he is working with and how it behaves in certain circumstances. To this end, when considering the person who will eventually be reading your comic story, the common denominator which you should be pursuing is not the lowest common denominator of public acceptability, but rather the denominator of basic humanity. If you're reading this, there's a fair chance that you're a human being. There's also a fair chance that no matter how unique and special you are or think you are, there are certain basic human mechanisms that you share with Conservative members of parliament, Yorkshire miners, radical lesbians and policemen. If you can identify and use these mechanisms to your own satisfaction, then you will have a much better basis for producing worthwhile art than if you'd spent your time hallucinating an imaginary average consumer and trying desperately to hammer your

work into a shape that will please his largely hypothetical tastes and criteria.

Okay, so now we have our basic idea and at least some idea of what sort of things are likely to most affect the broad spectrum of your readership. It is at this point that we can start to consider the actual form that the communication of our idea is to take. Before we get down to the finer details of the internal story mechanisms themselves, the first thing we have to consider is the story's basic shape and structure. In order to maximize the effect of the idea that you are trying to communicate it is preferable to give the story some form of defined shape so that it will have the right type of unity and sense of completeness to make a coherent and organized impression on the human mind. There are as many shapes for stories as there are shapes in nature. Some of them are irregular, and some of them are regular, all of them have their own advantages, drawbacks and possibilities. Presumably, you will choose a structure that seems to best suit the effect you want your story to have, but beyond that it doesn't really matter which structure you choose. The important thing is that you **understand** the structure of the work you are creating, whatever that structure might turn out to be. If you choose to deviate from it, then that's fine, just as long as you're aware of what you are doing and why you are doing it, and aware of its consequences upon the overall effect of the story.

Some structures are obvious and self-evident. One which I use a lot...probably far too much...is the basic elliptical structure, where elements at the beginning of the story mirror events which are to happen at the end, or where a particular phrase or a particular image will be used at the beginning and the end, acting as bookends to give the story that takes place in between a sense of neatness and unity. Another structure would be to start in the middle of the story and fill in the background at the same time as you progress the story into the future, thus moving both ways in time with the narrative at the same time. An example of this would be "A Time of Running" in *Swamp Thing* #26. The action starts in the middle, with Swamp Thing and Abby running through a swamp, and then fills in the events that have led up to that at the same time as we show the story continuing to evolve in the present. A more complex structure would be the one that I borrowed from Gabriel Garcia Marquez for the second part of "The Nukeface Papers" in *Swamp Thing* #36. Here, we have an entire story told by each character, depending on how much of the central action they happen to have seen individually. Thus, no one character has the whole story, but with each new character's retelling of events we find out a little more about the situation until finally we realize that the jigsaw is complete and the whole picture is finally before us, albeit unfolded in an unusual and hopefully interesting way. A simpler structure would be *Swamp Thing* #34, where the centerpiece of the issue was an eight-page erotic/abstract poem and the rest of the story was simply a frame for that centerpiece.

Even so, these are all mostly formal structures and there is no

reason why the aspiring comic writer should glean his notions of structure from a range as limited as my own. Returning again to Eddie Campbell, or indeed to Phil Elliot or Ed Pinsent or a number of other engaging talents that have emerged over the last few years outside the mainstream comic cattle-market, we find story shapes that are radically different from any of the more conservative forms described above. Campbell tends to give his stories a sort of informal anecdotal structure that mirrors precisely the way in which stories are usually recounted from person to person, with bits of backtracking and wandering away from the point left intact. The stories do have a precisely controlled structure, but it seems somehow far more natural and organic than a lot of the rather self-conscious structures that I use upon occasion. Phil Elliot has described his stories as having an "A" and a "B" to define the start and finish, with a sort of nonlinear and exploratory narrative taking place between those two points. These are all valid approaches, and looking at them with an analytical eye will certainly prove helpful in arriving at an idea of what structure actually is and what your own approach to the matter might be.

At this point, perhaps I ought to underline that even though I'm presenting these various story facets and elements in an order that seems to make sense to me, there is no reason why you should work out a story by taking the steps in the same order. Instead of starting with an idea you may decide that you have a nice idea for a story structure and then cast around for an idea that's suited to it. The episode of *V for Vendetta* entitled "Video," for example, was a story where the structure was conceived first: Is it possible to tell a story using only whatever incidental narration happens to be coming over a TV set? The structure led to the basic idea of the story, and when a suitable place arose in the ongoing *V* narrative into which the story might fit usefully, I used it. A single image, a single line of dialogue, any of these can be the point of origin for a story. My point is that somewhere along the line, wherever you choose to start, all of the various individual elements under discussion here will have to be examined if the work is going to be as good as you can possibly make it.

Now that we have some idea of structure, the next step is to consider the actual storytelling, which, for the purposes of discussion here, we will define as the way in which the story moves and behaves within the confines of the structure. Since we are now reaching the more well-defined areas of story composition, it's a lot easier to see the elements that go to make up the warp and weft of the storytelling process. In no particular order, prominent areas for consideration within the general grouping of "storytelling devices" include transition scenes, pacing, rhythm, smoothness of flow and all other aspects that relate more to the story itself than to the unfolding of events within that story.

Transitions, the movement between one scene and another, are one of the most tricky and intriguing elements of the whole writing process. The problem is to move from one place or one time to another without doing anything violent or clumsy that would disturb the reader's delicate thread of involvement in the story. If a transition is handled incorrectly, what it does is to bring the reader up short against the fact that he or she is reading a story. If you've spend the first scene building up the reader's involvement in the storyline and the characters, you don't want to do anything to remind him of their basic unreality. Since changes in location often require a sort of split-second pause between finishing one scene and beginning another, the transition gap is one of the places where you are most likely to lose your reader's interest if you don't handle it properly.

As I see it, a successful story of any kind should be almost like hypnosis: You fascinate the reader with your first sentence, draw them in further with your second sentence and have them in a mild trance by the third. Then, being careful not to wake them, you carry them away up the back alleys of your narrative and when they are hopelessly lost within the story, having surrendered themselves to it, you do them terrible violence with a softball bat and then lead them whimpering to the exit on the last page. Believe me, they'll thank you for it.

The important thing is that the reader should not wake up until you want them to, and the transitions between scenes are the weak points in the spell that you are attempting to cast over them. One way or another, as a writer, you'll have to come up with your own repertoire of tricks and devices with which to bridge the credibility gap that a change in scene represents, borrowing some devices from other writers and hopefully coming up with a few of your own. The one which I've used to excess, judging from a few of the comments I pick up in reviews or letter columns now and then, is the use of overlapping or coincidental dialogue. That said, it's a better trick to fall back on than the lame use of "Meanwhile, back at the ranch..." or some such similar utilitarian device, and it's more widely applicable than some of the more outre or experimental scene-change ideas, which often have only a limited application.

One thing I tend to do which eases the transition and is sometimes all that's needed to accomplish a good transition is to write in basic units of a single page, so that the reader's action in turning the page becomes the beat in which I change scene without disturbing the rhythm of the story. Another approach is to vary the "overlapping dialogue" technique and use a synchronicity of image rather than of words, or even just a coincidental linkage of vague abstract ideas. It's even possible to use color to change scene: The end of a scene which has a lot of gunplay and bloodshed might end with a close-up of the bright red blood all over the white floor. The next panel might suddenly cut to a marketplace in Italy and present a close-up of a flower trader's stall with a vast profusion of red blossoms taking up most of the panel. In that instance, the simple continuity of the color red could probably be enough to carry the reader successfully over the transition.

The transition doesn't always have to be smooth. If you're skillful enough you can sometimes manage a very abrupt transition with such style that no one will notice any break in flow until the moment has passed and they are safely absorbed in the next scene within the story. An example of this from the mine could be the stunning device that Hitchcock used in "The Birds": On finding a bird-ravaged body with the eyes pecked out, the heroine opens her mouth and sucks in a breath, obviously just about to let out an ear-splitting scream. Instead of showing us the scream, Hitchcock suddenly cuts to the next scene for a close-up of a motor suddenly screeching to life, the noise amplified and discordant so that it takes the place in the viewer's mind of the scream that they were expecting to hear the heroine let rip. The sudden change in scene is surprising, but Hitchcock manages to use the sense of surprise to positive ends, enhancing the enjoyment of the story rather than distracting from it.

This wouldn't work in the comic book medium, even with the use of lettered sound effects, but there's no reason why an enterprising mind shouldn't find a way to adapt the basics of the device to a sequence of words and pictures.

Transitions, while important in themselves, can also be considered as part of the general subject of pacing. Pacing, while if it's done correctly the reader will not even notice it, is an integral part of the story, determining the intellectual pace at which the reader will move through the story, and the timing of events within the story for greatest impact. The simplest and most mechanical way to understand comic book pacing is to work out how long a reader will spend looking at a panel before moving on to the next one. Firstly, they will spend a certain amount of time reading the captions and dialogue

balloons. A panel containing the standard 35 words of dialogue will take maybe seven or eight seconds to read, depending on the complexity of the image accompanying it. A simple graphic image without any captions or dialogue will maybe take three seconds. If you read a few comics with the pacing in mind you soon get a workable intuition for how long the reader will spend on each picture. While this doesn't give you anything like the rigid control of the time frame enjoyed by the film industry (which has its own disadvantages, as I pointed out last chapter) it does grant you some broad measure of control over how long it will take the reader's eyes to be guided through the page, or through the issue as a whole. Pacing should be geared toward the scene at hand. A thoughtful and pensive scene would probably work best with quite a slow pace. A fast action scene, maybe a fight scene, would very possibly work better if it moved as fast as possible. Compare some of Frank Miller's silent fight scenes—which move very fast, flowing from image to image with the speed of a real-life conflict, unimpeded by the reader having to stop to read a lot of accompanying text—and the fight scenes of lesser writers where any sense of movement in the scene is undercut by the antagonists mouthing huge chunks of dialogue at each other. The above are not meant to be hard and fast rules; I'm sure it's possible to write a fast-paced action scene and use lots of dialogue, and I know that it's possible by increasing the amount of detail in the actual pictures to do a long silent sequence that still reads very slowly. That said, some feel for how pacing works is essential to constructing a story, whether for purposes of building up suspense in a dramatic situation, or timing a gag in more comic circumstances. Play around with silent panels and see how they can be used to extend the moment of suspense over an extra beat, if necessary. Experiment with the idea of timing and see what comes up. In the Locas Tambien story "100 Rooms," Jaime Hernandez does some incredibly bold things with the time structure of his story and pulls them off with genuine élan. One example would be the scene where the embittered ex-nobleman who has "kidnapped" Maggie has just finally removed his hand from her mouth, confident that she isn't going to scream. Abruptly, in the very next panel, we cut to some unspecified time later within the same room. Maggie and the kidnapper have obviously just had sex and the man is sitting on the side of the bed apologizing for his behavior. This sudden abrupt and deliberate break in the pacing of the story is disorienting but somehow satisfying. It's nothing that I'd have dared to attempt personally, but it demonstrates just what is possible if you have sufficient talent and nerve and imagination. You can introduce elements that actually disturb the flow of your story and still get them to work in the context of the story as a whole.

Basically, there are no limits to the different storytelling effects and approaches that are possible, other than the limits imposed by one's own imagination. All that is required is that one should think about the techniques that one is using, and should understand them and know where they are applicable. Most importantly, it should always be born in mind that the various narrative devices are only there for the purpose of best conveying your story or some part of it. If you have a brilliant idea for a narrative device and it doesn't fit the story you're working on, leave it out. When the tricky narrative devices overwhelm the idea that you were trying to convey in the first place, then they are working to the detriment of the story rather than the benefit of it, and they must be ruthlessly expunged. As with most of the elaborately detailed waffle described above, the confidence over what to leave out and what to include in any given story are things that come only with practice and experience, but once you know what it is that you're looking for you'll probably find that it comes quicker than you expect.

CHAPTER THREE

WORLD BUILDING: PLACE AND PERSONALITY

Assuming that you now have some idea of the actual possibilities open to you in telling a story, then the next stage we move into concerns the elements within the actual work of fiction itself. For the sake of convenience, the main elements in this category can be broken down into three major areas: characterization, depiction of environment, and finally plot. Let's start with the environment first, because the nature of the plot and the motivations of the characters will be largely determined by the world in which they live.

The job of the writer, whether he or she is attempting to depict a colony on Neptune in the year 3020 or society life in London around 1890, is to conjure a sense of environmental reality as completely and as unobtrusively as possible. The most obvious way to do this is to explain the rudiments of your world to your readers by way of caption boxes or expository dialogue, but this is also to

my mind the most unnatural method and in many ways the least effective. It just happens to be the easiest, which is why it's used so often. Conversely, the best way to give your readers a sense of place and location in space and time is in my opinion the most difficult, while being the most rewarding in the long run.

If you look back to the early days of comics, when the writing was still pretty much in its infancy, you will come across many examples of a description of an environment by means of a brief caption or exposition. In the 30th century of the Legion of Super-Heroes, before Paul Levitz took over and began to put more effort into actually visualizing, along with Keith Giffen, the various worlds of the Legion's universe, most of the worlds were summed up in a couple of sentences. Matter-Eater Lad's planet of Bismoll was a world where all organic food was poisonous and so the inhabitants had learned how to eat inorganic substances of any kind. Little more than that was ever revealed, and that was deemed sufficient. All that's really needed is to show a couple of futuristic-looking buildings that appear pretty much the same as buildings on any other world in the 30th century and have a little caption explaining the dietary abnormalities of its inhabitants. Or at least, that was all that was needed to satisfy the readers of the early '60s. Since then, the rapid increment of information about our world available from the media has made even the younger readers all too painfully aware that a world is a complex place composed of many different interacting factors. A new approach to the problem that is more in keeping with contemporary perceptions seems to be required.

The best way, it seems to me, is to first consider the environment that you are working with as a whole, in detail, before ever putting pen to paper. Before writing *V*, for example, I came up with a mass of information about the world and the people in it, much of which will never be revealed within the strip for the simple reason that it isn't stuff that's essential for the readers to know and there probably won't be space to fit it all in. That isn't important. What is important is that the writer should have a clear picture of the imagined world in all its detail inside his or her head at all times. Returning to our Neptunian colony world for a moment, let's run through the sort of details which are essential to arriving at a clear picture of the world.

Firstly, how do human beings manage to live on Neptune? What are the physical problems that would

have to be overcome before people could live on such a world and what sound like feasible methods by which the difficulties could be solved? Might the fact that Neptune is largely made of gas necessitate a number of floating artificial environments, linked perhaps by a domestic teleportation network? How does the teleportation system work? What effect does the enormous gravity of the planet have upon the lives and the psychology of the people living there? What is the purpose of the Neptune colony? Is it perhaps mining materials for use on Earth? What are the political situations prevailing on Earth at this point in history and how do they affect the lives of the colonists? How long have the people been there? Have they been there long enough to properly develop their own separate culture? If so, what sort of paintings do they create and what sort of music do they make? Is it oppressive and claustrophobic art as a result of the pressures of living in such an enclosed environment, or are the pictures and pieces of music full of light and space to compensate for the inhibiting surroundings that the colonists are forced to endure? How is law maintained on the colony world? What sort of social problems exist? Are Earthmen the only species that has managed to colonize the world or are there any other alien races involved? Indeed, has mankind encountered any alien races at all in the decades leading up to the time our story is set or is he still alone in the universe as far as he knows? What does the economy work like on this place? How do people dress? How are the families set up?

This is the process I went through

have. Also, the story has the advantage of seeming much more natural since it follows almost exactly the way in which we perceive an alien culture if we happen to go abroad for our holidays. We don't necessarily understand everything about the culture straight away, but gradually as we pick up on the details surrounding us we get a complete sense of the whole of the environment, its unique atmosphere and the social elements which shape it. When a writer handles the environment in this way we don't get a sense of having a wealth of extraneous detail forced upon us just because the writer wants to let us know how thorough he's been in thinking it through. Instead we get a sense of a completely realized and credibly detailed world where things are still going on off-panel, even if the story isn't focusing upon them. A logically constructed world for your story to be set in will go a long way to suspending the disbelief of your readership and dragging them into the state of hypnosis that I mentioned in the last chapter.

While the comments above refer specifically to created environments, if you're tackling a place that actually exists you have to be every bit as thorough in your conception of the world that you are showing. When I started writing *Swamp Thing* I read up on Louisiana and the bayou as much as I had time for and managed to glean a just-about functional working knowledge of its plant and animal life, and general makeup. I know that water hyacinths form in a thick sheet upon the top of the water and make it appear to be solid ground, and that they grow so fast that at times in the past they have had to be practically

when coming up with the world of the Warpsmiths and the way their culture was constructed. I went through the same process with *Halo Jones* and *V for Vendetta*. The point is that once you have worked out the world in all its minute detail you are able to talk about it with complete confidence in a casual manner without hitting your reader over the head with a lot of exposition.

Howard Chaykin did it with *American Flagg*. He worked out the brand names and the TV shows and the attitudes to fashion and the political problems, and then he just went straight into his story and let the readers pick it up as they went along. In the first issue of *Flagg* we see snatches of TV shows and advertising billboards that give us a much more real impression of the way that these people think and live than any amount of explanatory caption boxes would burned out before they entirely overwhelmed the swamp. I know that alligators eat rocks, believing them to be turtles, and then are unable to digest them. This is why alligators have such shitty tempers. I know that the local Cajun Indians are referred to as "coonass" by the non-Cajuns as a type of racial slur and that the Cajuns have made a virtue of the insult by coming up with bumper stickers that read "Proud to be coonass." I know that the most popular Cajun name is Boudreaux. If I want a realistic-sounding name for an ordinary citizen of Louisiana I look in my Houma telephone directory until I come across one which strikes me as having a nice ring to it: Hattie Duplantis is a nice name. So is Jody Hebert. If I want to know which highway a character would have to take to get from Houma up to Alexandria I look it up in a gazetteer of the United States. It's the tiny little details like this that will make your depiction of a specific place convincing and realistic. They can be dropped casually into the pictures or the dialogue without fanfare and will probably be more convincing the more trivial and unimportant they seem to be.

Of course, when considering an environment it is not only the physical reality of the place that must be understood but also the emotional and atmospheric reality. Take Batman's Gotham City, for example. Is it just another version of New York? Is it a massive quaint playland for overgrown kids filled with giant typewriters and giant jack-in-the-boxes, populated by creatures like Bat-Mite and eccentrically malicious buffoons like the Penguin or the '50s Joker? Is it a dark and paranoid urban landscape straight out of Fritz Lang, terrorized by deformed freaks and monsters, where the only defender is a chilling and remorseless vigilante who dresses as a bat? The way in which you choose to treat the environment will alter the whole mood of the story, and it is as important to the final effect as an understanding of the actual physical factors which make up the world that you are writing about.

All right, so now we have our world. What sort of people live in it and how are we best to depict them? This brings us to the apparently highly problematical area of characterization.

The approach to characterization in comic books has evolved, like everything else in this retarded bastard medium, at a painfully slow pace over the last 30 or 40 years. The earliest approach found in comics was that of simple one-dimensional characterization, usually consisting of "This person is good" or "This person is bad." For the comics of the time and the comparatively simple world that they were attempting to entertain, this was perfectly adequate. By the early 1960s, however, times had changed and a new approach to characterization was needed. Thus, Stan Lee invented two-dimensional characterization: "This person is good but has bad luck with girlfriends," and "This person is bad but might just reform and join the Avengers if enough readers write in asking for it." Again, at the time this was breathtakingly innovative and seemed a perfectly good way of producing comics that had relevance to the times in which they were being produced. Progress since that point has been minimal. In an effort to keep up with the times, the characters themselves have become more extreme, brutal, bizarre or neurotic, but the basic way of portraying them has changed very little. They are still carefully defined two-dimensional characters, maybe with a little verbal window dressing thrown in to liven them up.

I think much of the blame for this state of affairs must rest in the largely unquestioning adherence to the dictum "If a character can't be summed up in 15 words then the character is no good." I mean, who says? While it's certainly possible to sum up the character and motivation of Captain Ahab in a well turned phrase like "This insane amputee with a grudge against a whale," Herman Melville obviously thought it appropriate to take slightly longer over the job. It seems to me that what is really meant by this largely spurious assertion is somewhat closer to "If a character can't be summed up in 15 words then it may not sell to an audience of young children, who we assume are of limited intelligence and possess brief attention spans".

Unwritten laws and conventional wisdoms of this nature really are the bane of the industry, or at least one of the banes of the industry. The problem is that they tend to trap people into a certain way of thinking about things. Obviously, if your character needs to be described in 15 words, you're going to aim at a 15-word character. Something along the lines of "A cynical police officer whose parents' murder leads him to wage masked war on crime." While this may well represent the beginnings of a perfectly workable character, the

tendency seems to be that the writer sees no further than that 15-word skeleton. Once or twice in every story, he will make sure that the character says something cynical and thinks back to his career as a police officer. Also, one of the supporting characters will probably say "Honestly! You're so cynical!!" To which our hero will reply, "What did you expect, babe? Remember, I used to be a police officer!" If the writer is comparatively skillful, minor quirks of personality will be introduced into the scheme. It is revealed, for example, that our cynical ex-police officer also collects stamps. Weirdly, this will usually be somehow tied back in to the initial 15-word premise: "Well, here I am, sitting with my album in front of me, licking hinges. Of course, I wouldn't be doing this if I were still a police officer. In fact, the more I think about the situation, the more cynical I feel."

If the writer is adventurous, he might feel the need to explore the character in greater depth. The problem is that however deep the pool of the character's soul might turn out to be it's still only 15 words wide. Maybe the writer will devote an entire issue to the character, attempting to unlock the mysteries of his past by means of a flashback or something. The story will have a central point and a theme, as stories should have, probably along the lines of "What was it that made this character so cynical?" Over the next 20 or so pages we run through the character's formative years, until we reach the apocalyptic event at the very core of the story. "I was just standing there, looking at my stamp album and the priceless collection that it had taken me years to build, when all of a sudden I realized that since I had foolishly pasted all of them directly into the album using an industrial-strength adhesive, they were completely worthless. I understood then that the universe was just a cruel joke upon mankind, and that life was pointless. I became completely cynical about human existence and saw the essential stupidity of all effort and human striving. At this point I decided to join the police force."

The point is that since the initial working assumptions upon which the characters are built are limited and increasingly unworkable, so too are the characters themselves. If comic writers are going to solve the problem of developing their level of characterization to a level where it's in keeping with the times, perhaps it wouldn't be a bad idea to throw away some of these outmoded templates and come at the problem from another angle. A logical place to start would be to simply go and look at some real people. Consider the character makeup of people around you and consider your own personality as well, in as cold and objective a light as is possible. After a little while you may discover that almost nobody can be summed up in 15 words, at least not in any meaningful or relevant way. You might also notice that people change their personality depending on whom they are talking to. They have a different voice in conversations with their parents from the voice that they use when addressing their workmates. They vary their attitude and their mood hour by hour. Often they will do things that seem completely out of character. Simple and unremarkable

observations such as these help to gear the creative mind toward a more complete understanding of characterization than can be afforded by any snappy little generalizations about the phenomenon.

It's worth looking at how people in other fields solve the problem of human verisimilitude. An artist who wants to learn how to realistically draw the human body will probably start out by drawing from life, observing the way that people stand and bend and move. Unless they are incredibly stupid they won't attempt to capture life by following a dubious pronouncement like "Good-looking figures all have big chins" or something of that nature.

Study yourself and the people around you in detail, and try to miss nothing...every little vocal tic and hesitation, every vague nuance of body posture or unconscious hand gesture. Listen to the way that they talk and try to re-create their voices in your head with all the quirks and mannerisms intact. While in all probability you will never in your entire career succeed in creating a character who is completely true to life, the effort will at least bring you nearer to this goal and to an understanding of the problems involved.

Another useful tool for characterization can be gleaned from the field of the theatre. I've mentioned before that I try to take a method-acting approach to characterization when possible, and it seems to yield reasonable results. As an example of how I'd approach a character by this method, I'd cite the way that the Demon was handled in issues #25-#27 of *Swamp Thing*. Working out the personality of Jason Blood presented no real difficulties, but since the Demon himself was actually meant to be a creature from Hell I realized that his psychology and inner workings would require some thought. I knew that he was a short and stocky character, and it struck me that he'd probably be enormously dense and tough, just as a result of living and surviving in Hell on a day-to-day basis. I imagined his weight to be massive, as if he were made of solid iron, and his internal body temperature to be roughly as hot as magma. This suggested a sort of feverish intensity in his thoughts and actions, along with a crushingly heavy and earthbound mass as a result of his sheer density.

I noticed that in Steve and John's original sketches for their proposed treatment of the character the fangs were more pronounced and the mouth has a slightly cat-like cleft in the upper lip. This suggested that the voice of the character would be slightly malformed, the speech impeded by the deformation of the lip and teeth.

Armed with all this information, I closed the curtains of my workroom so that the neighbors wouldn't worry and send out for a social worker or anything, and then I tried to imagine what it would actually feel like to be that character. I imagined the immense weight of my body, which was now much smaller, and saw that this would give the movements of the body a sort of terrible momentum. In keeping with the feral nature suggested by the front teeth I tried out the sensation of hunching myself up like Quasimodo and squatting slightly as I walked. After I felt that I had the physical feel of the character I tried the voice, thrusting my front teeth out and curling my upper lip until it became difficult to talk clearly. Making any sort of sense at all seemed to necessitate talking very slowly, which suggested a sort of slowed-down gramophone quality to the voice, very deep and guttural. Eventually I realized that the exact voice I was looking for was a sort of electronically treated version of Charles Laughton's voice in "Mutiny on the Bounty." Having sorted out the voice and the posture of the character, you can fix the impression in your mind to summon up when the time comes around to put the character through their paces and producing realistic dialogue for them to speak.

One conclusion I've come to is that almost everybody has a practically infinite number of facets to their personality but chooses to focus upon no more than a handful for most of the time. We all have areas within ourselves that are cruel, mean-spirited, cowardly, lecherous, violent, greedy... if describing a character with those attributes we must be prepared to look in the eye the areas of our personality that we feel least comfortable with and make an honest appraisal of what we see. Conversely, all of us have sides that are noble, heroic, unselfish or loving, whether we care to admit to them or not. In creating a noble character, you should first try to see whatever spark of nobility there might be in you, however unlikely the prospect of its existence might be during your bleaker moments.

The more adventurous you become with characterization, the more confident you become about tackling some of the more specific and knotty problems of the craft. As a white male writer, for example, and a practicing heterosexual, how am I to write about a homosexual character, or a Black character, or a woman? Theoretically, of course, it should be easier to write about people of another race, gender or sexual inclination than about sentient vegetable consciousness, alienated ubermenschen or creatures from the pit. Where this comes unstuck is that if you get the characterization of your walking vegetable wrong, you aren't going to offend anybody or hurt anybody or misrepresent anybody that actually exists. Dealing with the vast multitude of different character types that you'll probably create in the course of your writing career is at once absorbing and demanding. One day you'll be a child murderer in New York, the next a sentient crystalline creature on Altair 4, the next a 70-year-old nun working with the survivors of a second plague of London during the year 2237. You'll be forced to consider people who are either politically or morally offensive to you and try to understand them.

This can sometimes be personally, as well as professionally rewarding, but the main result is that in writing about characters during the course of your work you will take the right degree of care and aspire to the required degree of authenticity or stylization with a complete grasp of the principles involved. Remember that everybody in the story is a character, even if they only happen to stroll across the background without speaking and are never seen again. Every time you commence a story you are creating a world and populating it. Even if you can't afford to take the time to spend the customary seven days over this every time, you should at least make sure that you give it as much thought as is necessary.

CHAPTER FOUR

THE DETAILS; PLOT AND SCRIPT

Now that we have our idea, our structure, our approach to storytelling, our environment and our characters sorted out, I suppose we might as well think about coming up with a plot (although as you may have gathered if you've read much of my work I very often can't be bothered with this formality). So, what the hell is a plot? What does it look like?

One thing that might be helpful to muse upon is what a plot **isn't**. A plot isn't the main point of the story or the story's main reason for existing. It is something that is there more to **enhance** the central idea of the story and the characters who will be involved in it than to dominate them and force them to fit its restrictions. Coming up with a straightforward mechanical plotline isn't difficult at all, and there are plenty of tried and tested formulas to fall back on, especially within the comic industry. What **is** difficult is to come up with a plot worthy of a reaction stronger than "So what?" The words "So what?" are an almost magical incantation that will reveal whether your plot ideas really have what it takes to actually reach an audience and say something to them.

Gamma Man escapes from prison and runs amok, intent on taking revenge upon his arch-foe Really Terrific Man. After a prolonged fight, Really Terrific Man understands that if he can cut Gamma Man off from the gamma rays that are the source of his power, his foe will weaken and collapse. He melts down some lead pipes from the plumber's yard where they happen to be fighting and pours the molten lead over the indestructible Gamma Man, who immediately freezes to motionlessness, leaving Really Terrific Man the victor. So what? Really Terrific Man is worried that his powers are gradually fading away just when Gamma Man bursts out of the block of lead six issues later seeking hideous revenge, but by the end of that issue the fluke sunspot activity that caused his temporary lack of might has passed, allowing him to beat the shit out of Gamma Man and then imprison him at the Earth's core. So what? Really Terrific Man is in love with the cleaning woman who tidies up his secret fortress for him, but he daren't ask her to marry him in case this makes her a target for his enemies. So what?

What seems to me to be a disproportionate amount of effort is expended on coming up with madly elaborate plots involving dozens of characters, these plots having no relevance at all to anything other than themselves. Pick up an average current comic and put it to your ear and you can almost hear the process at work: Plot, plot, plot, plot, plot, plot...it sounds like someone wading through mud and it very often reads like it, too. An obsession with the demands of a concrete and linear plotline is often one of the most dependable ways to crush all the life and energy from your story and make it simply an exercise in mechanical narration.

Naturally, while I'd like to point out that to overemphasize the importance of the plot may be ultimately destructive to the work as a whole, there are obviously some stories that demand a more complex plot. Using different examples from my own work I'd refer you to a couple of the "Time Twisters" that I did for *2000 AD*. One of them, "The Reversible Man," had no plot at all other than a straightforward recounting of a totally average life with all of the events in reverse order. The other story, "Chronocops," had

one of the most complex plots that I've come up with in my career thus far, due to the necessity to work several convoluted time paradoxes into the story so that it could still be read and enjoyed in a coherent fashion.

What I'm trying to say is that there **are** some stories where the plot **will** be the most important thing, its ingeniousness and the skilled execution of its twists and turns being the thing that excites the reader. A lot of short science-fiction stories are plot-oriented, at least as that genre is represented in comics, along with other short story formats such as the horror yarn as treated by EC and its many imitators. Most murder mysteries are almost entirely plot-oriented, and no one would deny that the fiction of Raymond Chandler counts Chandler's exquisite plotting as one of its greatest assets. Obviously, a knowledge of plot is important. It simply mustn't be allowed to dominate the entire work in an unhealthy way, nor be seen in such rigid and restricting linear terms. Returning to the example of Chandler, even though plotting was one of his strong points he never allowed it to dominate and subvert the entire story. The thing that one is left with after reading, say, *The Big Sleep*, is not so much a detailed memory of the turns of the plot but rather a vivid picture of a weary but unflinchingly moral character trying to come to terms with a moral twilight world where no one ever seems to have all their cards on the table and where lies and half-truths and threats become the main social currency. Chandler's **point** in most of his fiction seems to be in conveying this

sense of the world through the perceptions of Philip Marlowe or whoever. The plot is there as something more to move the reader's interest through this world, taking in the sights, and to provide an illustration of the way events seem to work in this harsh and treacherous landscape.

So, given that a plot is important, how does one go about coming up with one? The best answer that I have come across to date is the same answer that applies to most of the questions that have been raised during this ramble: Look at the whole thing, and try to see the whole shape before you attempt to get down to specifics and describe the parts. What is a plot? A plot is the combination of environment and characters with the single element of time added to it. If the combination of environment and characters can be called "the

situation," then plot is a situation as seen in four dimensions.

Using an example that I've borrowed from Brian Aldiss' excellent "Report on Probability A," let's think about something other than comics to give us a different perspective on the idea. Let's consider a specific painting. The painting is *The Hireling Shepherd* by the Pre-Raphaelite William Holman Hunt.

In this painting, we see a woman sitting facing us in the foreground with a beautiful and luminous pastoral landscape behind her, bathed in the golden light of late afternoon. Crouching or kneeling just behind the woman we see a young man, the hireling shepherd of the title. He has one of his arms raised behind her shoulder, as if he is about to establish physical intimacy by wrapping the arm around her. However, at the moment depicted in the painting his hand has not yet touched her. Trapped in the palm of the hand there is a tiny death's-head moth. The expressions of both the handsome shepherd and the young woman are ambiguous. The shepherd seems lustful while the woman seems coquettish. Seen in another light his expression is slightly more sinister while hers becomes one of suppressed alarm. Behind the pair, in the gold-drenched English fields, a herd of sheep wander about aimlessly, untended and unprotected while the shepherd dallies with the young beauty on the grassy ridge up above their pasture. The shepherd seems to smile as he prepares to show the young woman the death's-head moth, and she doesn't seem displeased by this advance. The sheep graze, the moth flutters, the moment is frozen, with neither past nor resolution. It's a single second taken out of a story of which we know nothing else. We do not know anything of the previous lives of these characters: We don't know where the shepherd grew up or even where he spent the previous night. We don't know if the woman just happened to chance by that way or whether she had previously agreed to meet the young man at that spot.

Of their future we know even less. When he shows her the moth will she be enchanted or repulsed? Will they make love, or just talk, or perhaps argue? What will become of the sheep, left untended? With an eye to the seemingly ominous symbolism of the death's-head moth, is something darker implied? Not necessarily something melodramatic like the possibility that the shepherd is about to strangle the girl, but maybe some comment on mortality and the ways in which we squander the substance of our lives? Is this eternal moment that we see, captured from the canvas, a moment from the beginning of a relationship or the end of same? The beauty of a good painting is that the mind and feelings can wander endlessly around inside it, following their own paths and moving at their own pace through the timeless place that the painting represents. *The Hireling Shepherd* shows us a situation. The situation does not change or move, but we ourselves may move around within it, mentally, enjoying the subtle shifts in perspective and meaning.

Now, if we add the dimension of time to that situation, the work of art is completely altered. Instead of having infinite possibilities, if the situation in the painting is to progress through time it must follow only one route. The structuring of events along this route is a plot. The girl in the painting notices the death's-head moth and is both intrigued and a little frightened by it. Led thus into conversation with the charismatic hireling shepherd, the woman finds herself equally fascinated by him. They make love, after first setting free the moth. After their lovemaking is done they discover that the herd of sheep have been stolen or spirited away during the interim. Rather than face the wrath of the irate farmer who had hired him to tend the sheep, the footloose, drifting worker decides to leave the neighborhood without reporting the theft and seek employment in the next county. After a number of weeks, the woman realizes she is pregnant. Her father and brothers learn of this and swear to track down the hireling shepherd and offer him a choice of marriage or death…and so on and so on. Admittedly, the above is a clumsy and ugly extrapolation with none of the poetry or charm or subtlety of the original painting, but I think it makes the point that plotting is a sort of four-dimensional phenomenon, taking time to be the fourth dimension. The situation shown in the painting is a representation of a three-dimensional world that with the addition of time becomes four-dimensional and changes from a situation into a plot.

Thus, to consider the plotting process in any worthwhile way you must try to think in four-dimensional terms. See the world that your characters inhabit as a continuum with a past, a present and a future. See the shape of the whole thing, and you will be more able to see how the elements within that overall design relate to each other with much greater clarity. *Watchmen* was conceived in precisely this way. The story starts in October 1985 and ends a few months later. In terms of real time, that is the framework of the story, and I have all of the events within that period precisely worked out. In broader terms, however, the story concerns events going as far back as 1940, with individual sequences set in the '60s, the '70s, the '50s, the '40s...what we get an impression of, hopefully, is a world with a credible sense of depth and history, along with characters that share the same quality. In being able to see a 45-year sweep of history relating to the world my story is set upon before ever attempting to write a single syllable about that world, I'm given the advantage of being able to notice patterns of events and events which somehow mirror each other conceptually, interesting potential elements of the story and its telling that I can bring out as the story progresses. I notice opportunities to tie together elements of the plot or the thematic structure of the book and present a more coherent and effective whole as a result. Also, since I have the history of the world and its various characters mapped out in advance, I will perhaps notice an interesting juxtaposition of characters or events which would logically happen at some point in the story and which suggest an interesting scene or piece of action or exchange of dialogue.

Establish your continuum as a four-dimensional shape with length, breadth, depth and time, and then pick out the single thread of narrative that leads you most interestingly and most revealingly through the landscape that you've created, whether it be a literal landscape or some more abstract and psychological terrain. This thread of narrative is your plot. As the plot moves through the well-visualized continuum that you have created for it to exist in, you will find that it's easy to get a realistic and nicely underplayed impression of a whole real world going on beyond the confines of the actual story that we happen to be telling. Just by knowing all the trivial little details regarding the continuum containing your central stream of narrative, you will find that the essential minor elements that give a story a credible context to exist in will find a way naturally into your narrative without the need to be forced. A good example of this would be the worlds that Jaime and Gilbert Hernandez created for their major contributions to *Love and Rockets*. In Jaime's "Locas Tambien" and "Mechanics" storylines we have a sense of a whole mass of credible detail hovering just beyond the borders of the panels and the confines of the story itself. After seeing the name referred to in various bits of graffiti for months we finally learn that "Missiles of October" is the name of Hopey's band in just the same casual way that we find out that her second name is Glass or that Maggie's auntie, Vicky Glori, once had a hotly contested championship bout with Rena Titanon during Titanon's wrestling days. In "Heartbreak Soup" Gilbert has done an equally impressive job on his depiction of the community of Palomar over a period of 15 or 20 years of story time. We see Jesus and Heraclio and Vicente and the others grow up and settle into their own distinctive adult lifestyles. We see Sheriff Chello start her career as a Banadora ("a woman who washes men") before being squeezed out of business by the beautiful Luba and being forced to take to law enforcement. In later sequences we see how perfectly she has taken to her new vocation and we see that she is gradually becoming slimmer and more attractive, even as Luba starts to look increasingly strained and conscious of how much she misses the freedom of her youth, along with an awareness perhaps of the passing of her beauty. The world is real and three-dimensional. It takes 15 years of story time before we start to realize that Vicente is more upset by his disfigurement than he originally seemed to be. We watch as children with different mothers, both sired by the since-deceased young heartthrob Manuel, playing together during a public feast and holiday while grown-up life goes on all about them. We have a sense of a complete continuum, within which everything takes on its own degree of importance and becomes a vital part of the overall work of art.

All right...in the previous Lord knows how many pages, we have considered different approaches to structure, storytelling, environment and characterization along with the nature of a plot and the importance of a central idea. Bearing all of the above notions in mind, we can finally proceed to start work on the script itself.

We have an idea we wish to communicate and a plot that underlines and reveals the idea in an interesting way. We have solid, rounded characters for the story to happen **to** and an equally solid and credible world for it to happen **in**. The first step is to take our story, which presumably we will have arrived at with an eye to how many pages are available to print it in, and see exactly how well it fits into the given restrictions that we have. As an example for how this process works, I'd cite 1985's *Superman* Annual #11. The idea behind the story was to examine the concept of escapism and fantasy dreamworlds, including happy times in the past that we look back on and idealize, and longed-for points in the imagined future when we will finally achieve whatever our goal happens to be. I wanted to have a look at how useful these ideas actually are and how wide the gap is between the fantasy and any sort of credible reality. It was a story, if you like, for the people I've encountered who are fixated upon some point in the past where things could have gone differently or who are equally obsessed with some hypothetical point in the future when certain circumstances will have come to pass and they can finally be "happy." People who say, "If only I hadn't married that man or that woman. If only I'd stayed in college, left college earlier, settled down, gone off to see the world, got that job I turned down..." or who say, "When the mortgage is paid off, then I can enjoy myself. When I'm promoted and I get more money, then I can have a good time. When the divorce comes through, when the kids are grown up, when I finally manage to get my novel published...." These people are

so enslaved by their perception of the past and future that they are incapable of properly experiencing the present until it's vanished.

The plot that I chose to get that idea across involved Superman's mind being enslaved by an organic telepathic parasite that fed him an illusion of his heart's desire…a planet Krypton that never blew up. This is part of a plot by Superman's alien enemy Mongul, who wants Superman out of the way so that he can take over the universe or whatever these tyrant types usually aspire to. The story takes place on Superman's birthday, in the Fortress of Solitude, with simultaneous sequences going on inside Superman's mind as he imagines himself on the world of Krypton as it would have been if it had never exploded. In the course of the story, we see that such an eventuality might

not have been as happy as it looks at first glance, finally leading Superman to throw off the fantasy and see it for what it is. At the same time he sees his useless nostalgia for a vanished planet as it really is, and learns something about himself from the experience.

Okay…so the problem is how to present that plot and its attendant idea within the restrictions that are imposed by the length of the book, the market it is aimed at and so forth. The most immediate and concrete restriction is that the book is 40 pages long. This means that I must fit my story into that precise length without it appearing either crammed or padded out unnecessarily. Thus, my first step is usually to take a piece of paper and write the numbers one to 40 down the left-hand side. I then start to sketch in the scenes about which I already have some ideas and try to work out how many pages they will take up.

I've already worked out that I want to present a contrast between the world of Krypton in Superman's dreams and the external reality of his situation, standing paralyzed in the Fortress of Solitude with an alien fungus clinging to his chest and feasting from his bio-aura. In order for this to work, I need something interesting to be going on in the Fortress of Solitude while Superman is asleep, so that I can cut between an involving scene in the dreamworld and an equally engaging scene taking place simultaneously in the "real world." Since in terms of the plot it happened to be Superman's birthday, it seemed logical that a couple of his superhuman pals might be visiting and provide the opportunity for some interesting incidental conflict with Mongul, the villain of the piece, who is also visiting the Fortress to survey his handiwork. Given all this, I sat down and worked out a sequence of events that appeared logical and that described what happened to Superman's chums (Wonder Woman, Batman and Robin, as it turned out; I originally wanted to use Supergirl but then Julie Schwartz informed me that she'd be popping her bright red clogs during *Crisis on Infinite Earths* and suggested that I use Wonder Woman instead) from their arrival at the Fortress bearing presents for Superman.

The rough schematic would run something as follows: They arrive, and we establish their characters in a few brief strokes and show how they react to each other. With their dialogue, we establish the basic situation, and let the reader know that it's Superman's birthday. We establish that both Wonder Woman and the Dynamic Duo have brought gifts—Wonder Woman has a large parcel that she refuses to disclose the contents of, while Batman and Robin have had a special rose named "The Krypton," bred in honor of the occasion. Upon entering the Fortress, they find Superman with a strange growth of black roses seemingly growing from his chest. He is immobile and totally insensate. While they are trying to figure out what's going on, Mongul announces his presence and reveals the rest of the salient plot details both to the three superheroes and to the readers. Wonder Woman attempts to tackle him and is singled out for a brutal beating which knocks her across the trophy hall of the Fortress and

through the wall into the weapons room, where the alien weaponry proves useless against Mongul. Meanwhile, Batman is coolly trying to revive Superman as the only real hope of saving the situation. More as a result of Superman's growing disenchantment with the fantasy world he is in than by Batman's efforts, the black-rose creature comes loose and grabs hold of Batman instead. It is at this point, freed from the creature's influence, that Superman wakes up. The fantasy he has been living through is over and the two strands of narrative merge into one again as events start to build towards the issue's climax.

Okay...now having worked that out I had to work out a similar schematic of events concerning the happenings inside Superman's skull: We open in Kryptonopolis, where we establish that Superman is living as Kal-El, who has a wife and two children and works long and tiring hours as an archaeologist. We learn that Krypton seems to be in a state of social decline, having passed the peak of its civilization. Kal-El's father, Jor-El, has been spurned by the science community since his predictions concerning the doom of Krypton proved to be unfounded, and with the death of his wife Lara he has become a frustrated and embittered old man who flirts with extremist political groups in an attempt to halt the decline that he sees in the standards of Kryptonian life. This brings him into conflict with his more liberal son, and the two have become estranged. We see events start to come to a head as we learn that Kal-El's cousin, Kara, has been attacked and wounded by armed members of a group campaigning for the abolition of the Phantom Zone and bearing a grudge against anyone even remotely related to that device's inventor, Jor-El. Alarmed by this development we see Kal-El and his family attempting to flee Kryptonopolis against a backdrop of torchlight parades, riots and demonstrations as Krypton starts to slide faster and faster towards collapse. Finally, Kal can no longer accept the terms of the fantasy, and is no longer prepared to pay the miserable price required in order to sustain it. He breaks free of the fantasy to find Batman is now a prisoner of the plant that induced the dream, as the two strands of narrative bond together.

The next step was to try to integrate these sequences into a coherent whole, so that they ran in parallel for the first approximate half of the 40-page book. This meant that I had to allocate so many pages to Superman's fantasy and so many pages to the scenes inside the Fortress with Batman and company, deciding roughly what went on each page with an eye to making each page roughly a complete scene in itself. I knew that all this stuff needed to go at the beginning of the book, covering the first 25 or so sides. This meant that I must intercut between the two strands of narrative at well-timed junctures and try to bring both strands toward the boil at roughly the same time. In establishing a good beginning for the story I had an immediate choice: Either I could start with the arrival of the visiting superheroes or I could dump the reader straight in at the deep end without any explanation by starting with Superman's fantasy. Since it seemed more likely that this

latter course would tend to surprise and intrigue the reader, I chose to open with a scene set upon the illusory Krypton of Superman's parasite-induced imaginings. Hopefully, the effect upon the reader should have been something along the lines of "Huh? Where are we? On Krypton? But Krypton exploded. Is this story happening in the past? Nope—there's Kal-El, and he's the same age he is now, but he looks sort of different. He looks ordinary, and he's wearing glasses and he has a straight job and a wife and a couple of kids. What's going on here?" If this first page is sufficiently intriguing, then you've gone a long way towards hooking the reader. Having established the basic situation upon this imaginary Krypton, we turn over the page and cut straight to the Arctic Circle, for the arrival of Superman's three birthday visitors. As they pursue a hopefully natural and yet casually revealing dialogue, they make their way into the Fortress. Since I'm aware that pages 2 and 3 are on left-hand and right-hand pages respectively, it would seem advantageous to save any big visual surprise until page 4, so that the reader doesn't see it until he turns over. Thus, page 3 ends with a teaser. Having entered the Fortress, the three heroes are staring at us in surprise and dawning horror, looking at something off-panel that we cannot see. This hopefully suggests something sufficiently intriguing to get the reader to turn the page over to page 4. Since there's an ad break immediately after page 4 and since I quite like having a full-page splash panel, just to give the title of the story and its suggested premise some weight and moment and to signify that the story has started in proper, page 4 is the splash. Thus, on the fourth page, we see what Batman and Robin and Wonder Woman are seeing: Superman, standing there frozen with a hideous black-red growth spilling from his breast. With any luck, the reader is intrigued by this unusual state of affairs enough to move past the ad for Fig Newtons and Apple Newtons to page 5 of the story overleaf, where we have a page showing the reactions of Superman's buddies as they try to find out what's wrong with their comrade. The page ends with a close-up of Superman's face staring out of the foreground at us while Batman, standing behind him, remarks that he's in a world of his own. We move our eyes upward to the top of page 6.

Here, we have an image that echoes the picture in the previous panel. Once more, Kal-El stares out of the foreground at us, but now we are back on Krypton, in Superman's dream, quite literally in "a world of his own." Thus, the coincidence of images and the irony of Batman's remark provide a smooth and semi-meaningful transition between the two scenes without losing the readers' attention. On page 6 we show the relationship between Kal-El and his wife with some degree of additional detail and use their dialogue to fill in the reader regarding a little of what their situation is. The page ends with a nighttime shot of their apartment building against a beautiful blue and pink night sky, immediately after Kal has mentioned going to see his father the next day.

We turn the page and we have a shot looking up at a different Kryptonian building, this time with a

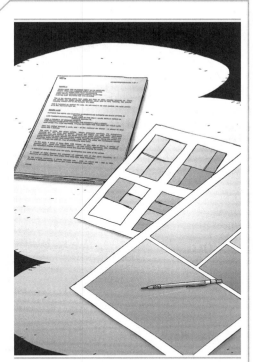

red, yellow and orange morning sky behind it. We are obviously still on Krypton, and it is just as obviously the morning of the following day. We then run through a three-page confrontation between Kal El and his embittered father that ends on page 9 with Jor-El smashing out in futile anger at one of the ornamental glass trees on his terrace and shattering a petrified glass bird, frozen in the act of feeding its young. The last shot is of the parent bird's snapped-off glass head, a glass worm still held in its beak. Even as this provides an image symbolic of the break in the father-son relationship between Kal-El and his old man, it ties in obliquely with the overlapping caption box affixed to that panel. This is a sort of voice-over from the following scene reading, "Really, it's just a matter of putting the pieces together," this sentence actually relating to

Batman's comment on the deductive process as applied to finding out what's wrong with Superman but also having apparent relevance to the image of the broken bird lying there in pieces that are impossible to put back together. This leads us into page 10, which commences a four-page scene in which Mongul arrives and picks a fight with Wonder Woman. It ends with Mongul saying, "Thank you. I think that's answered my question," while reaching for Wonder Woman as in the background Superman stands immobile looking on, his eyes unseeing. On the next page we have a scene back on Krypton, at the hospital. In the foreground, we have Supergirl's mother, Allura. In the background, in roughly the same position relative to the foreground figures as he was in the preceding panel, Kal-El is entering the hospital from the dark city outside. Allura, desperately quizzing a nurse about her daughter's condition, says "I asked you a question." This continues in a similar fashion, cutting back and forth by various methods, until we reach page 25 and the awakening of Superman.

Having mapped out the first half of the book, I was able to see how much space I had to get in the things that needed to happen at the end. I knew, for example, that I needed a good strong last page, preceded by a couple of pages just spent dealing with the aftermath of the action and establishing a mood of returned normality and reflection upon the lessons that have been learned. This took up roughly four pages at the end. This meant that pages 26 to 36 were left for the final climactic battle between Superman and Mongul,

which seemed about the right sort of length.

Using the same rough procedures as above, I then broke down this 10-page action sequence into a hopefully interesting flow of minor events as Superman and Mongul paste each other around the interior of the Fortress. To work this out, I referred extensively to an already established schematic of the Fortress loaned to me by Dave "Fanboy' Gibbons. I knew that Superman would first come upon Mongul in the weapons room, where the giant alien was still beating up Wonder Woman. If Mongul punched Superman hard enough to drive him upwards through the ceiling, he would end up in the alien zoo, immediately above. Knocking each other along the length of the zoo, they would push through into the communications room with its computer archives. If at this point they managed to smash each other through the floor they would find themselves sprawled on the ground in front of the giant statue of Jor-El and Lara holding the globe of Krypton between them, which is immediately below. This seemed like a good place to conclude the battle, with its inherent echo of the world that Superman spent the first half of the story imagining. At the same time as this is going on, we follow the progress of Robin as he tries to both help out and also to get Superman to help him work out what to do with the writhing organism that Robin has by now pried off Batman. He follows the path of destruction that Superman and Mongul have left behind them during their battle, finally happening upon the pair in time to provide the vital element needed to defeat

Mongul. Again, this had to be done naturally, simultaneously bringing both strands of narrative (Robin/parasite and Superman/Mongul) to a head.

Mongul is finally subdued by the organism with which he had intended to trap Superman. After a three-page aftermath in which the heroes relax and chat after the battle we have Batman presenting his specially bred "Krypton" rose, which had been crushed and killed during the fighting. Superman calmly accepts the death of the rose, and by extension the death of Krypton, providing a neat emotional point at which to bring the story to a close with the central idea explored and at least partially resolved. The final page, mirroring the first page of the whole story, lets us have a glimpse into the terrible and blood-thirsty dream reality conjured by Mongul under the parasite's influence, showing that he is more hopelessly trapped within his own dreams than Superman ever could be, and providing a counterpoint to Superman's eventual success with his eventual failure.

Fine. Now we have the story completely broken down with an understanding of more or less exactly what goes on each page and in each panel and in each scene, along with an understanding of how all the disparate elements that we've considered are working together to form the whole. The only remaining stages are the purely creative final processes of arriving at the correct stream of both verbal and visual narrative. By verbal narrative I mean the exact choice of words and the flow of language that will take the reader through the story upon one level and the precise flow of imagery that will take him or her through the book upon another level.

The fine craft of wordsmithing is important in that clumsy or boring or lifeless language stands a high chance of distracting the reader from the story that you're trying to tell. You first learn how to use words to the best of your ability, once more applying real thought to the processes involved. What, for example, separates an interesting sentence from a dull one? It's not the subject matter...a good writer can write about the most mundane object in the world and make it interesting. It's something in the arrangement of words that brings the whole structure alive with meaning and makes a powerful impression upon the reader, not in the content of those words. By looking at sentences in the works of others that have appealed to you—whether in a poem or a novel or a comic—it's possible to see certain patterns that follow similar basic principles to phenomena that we've discussed earlier: The element of surprise is very often the most appealing thing about a sentence... the surprising use of a word, or the surprising juxtaposition of two interesting concepts. Using an example that I personally quite liked but which most people seem to find an example of my overwriting at its worst, there was a line in an early *Swamp Thing* about clouds like plugs of bloodied cotton wool dabbing uselessly at the slashed wrists of the sky. This was a description of a sunset, and the intention was to

sound even if the actual execution left something to be desired.

Along with the surprise content of the language and the concepts in each sentence, there is verbal rhythm to consider. A sentence overloaded with long, multi-syllable words, for example, would probably have a very jerky and unsatisfactory stumbling kind of rhythm in the reader's head as he or she reads the line, and even more so if they attempt to read it aloud. Be conscious of the rhythm in your writing and of the effect that it has on the tone of your narrative. Long, flowing sentences with lots of lush imagery will have one effect. Short, sparse sentences delivered in machine-gun fashion will have another. Sometimes, repeating a phrase or a word will give a sequence a rhythm almost like music, where various musical phrases are repeated throughout a piece to lend it structure. Each word-rhythm has its own attributes, and there is an infinite number of different rhythms to be discovered by someone with enough imagination.

Dialogue, as spoken in word balloons, should also have its own individual rhythm, depending on the character delivering it. An excellent rule of thumb for dialogue is to read it aloud and see if it would sound natural enough to deliver in conversation without your friends looking at you in a peculiar fashion and wondering why you're talking so funny. Most comic book dialogue doesn't pass this test. Read it out aloud and it sounds phony and ridiculous. By developing an ear for dialogue and being aware of the principles involved, it is fairly simple to avoid this trap and produce

describe a thing of unquestioned beauty in very ugly and sordid and depressing terms. I found the juxtaposition of the two sensations stimulating and entertaining, but apparently for a lot of people it crossed over the line into self-parody, which smacks of bad judgment upon my part, but probably something I shall do again and again for the rest of my career. Creating a single story requires that you make thousands and thousands of tiny creative decisions on the basis of whatever theories you hold dear and the application of large measures of intuition. Much as I would it were otherwise, nobody gets it right all the time, and if you have made a mistake the only thing you can do is analyze it, see if you agree with your critics and respond accordingly. Adverse reaction aside, I still believe that the principle of surprise behind the sentence referred to above is interchanges of dialogue or first-person soliloquies that are authentic and convincing and natural.

The visual narrative of a strip is simply what goes into the pictures. For this, it is vital that a writer thinks visually and takes advantage of how much information it is possible to casually convey within an image without overburdening either the picture with extraneous detail or the captions with lengthy descriptions. Even if your drawing ability is as minimal as my own, it's fairly easy to arrive at a developed visual sensibility by getting into the habit of doing rough thumbnail layouts of each page before you write it, showing the visual elements that go in each panel. You will glean an idea of what it's possible for an artist to show within a panel, and you'll get some notion of how the completed page will hang together in terms of composition: Are there too many full-facial close-ups or full-figure shots? Are they all seen from the same boring angle? Would this panel in the middle where you want to establish a sense of menace be better if it were viewed from directly above, so that we get an almost subliminal sense of something looking down upon the unsuspecting characters below, ready to pounce? Does this four-panel sequence slowly zooming in on the character's eyes take up too much space and upset the page's balance? Would it be better as a three-panel sequence instead, using the leftover panel for something else? Is there too much information crammed into this panel, and if so is there room on the page to split it into two panels so that it reads more smoothly? Considerations of this sort will allow

you to at least provide a workable visual structure for the piece which is coherent and clear enough for the artist to understand the effect you are after and the purpose behind it, and to use as a solid jumping-off point for whatever visual input he or she may care to add to the art and design, bearing in mind that the artist will almost certainly have visual sensibilities 50 times more sound and reliable than your own.

Also, an ability to think visually will allow you to plan the inclusion of numerous small subliminal elements that will greatly enhance the reader's peripheral enjoyment of the story. With a little imagination, it's possible to have tiny events going on unimportantly in the foreground or the background of a picture, seemingly with no relevance to the main story but providing the reader with a subliminal reinforcement of the ideas being discussed in the actual narrative. The reader does not have to notice these elements consciously in order to be affected by them, and it's an excellent if sneaky way of increasing the reader's enjoyment of your story and getting your point over forcefully without being long-winded or intrusive. In the two-part *Vigilante* story that I did (#17 and #18), for example, there's a scene where the Vigilante and Fever, the female lead character, are driving around the city while Fever is giving the Vigilante an impromptu and somewhat sweeping lecture on the evils of authority and the effect it has on society. As the car drives through the city I asked Jim Baikie to include some unobtrusive bits of background business showing authority in action. In one panel a police officer cautions some street punks sitting on the hood of a car. In the next a mother shouts angrily at her reluctant and wailing child. In the next a priest wags his finger at a doubtful-looking elderly woman. All of these incidental details, while unimportant in themselves, add a sort of extra resonance to the things being said in the frame, increasing the story's sense of reverberation.

And that, basically, is that. Having finished your story, go back and see if there are any bits that need changing, and make the last few minor adjustments necessary to give the right degree of polish. Your comic strip is as good as you're going to get it and you must wait for long months to see whether the readers think so too, often a very irritating and nail-chewing time when you find yourself going through violent mood swings in which you alternately consider the work to be amongst the best you've ever done and then a day later conclude that it's nothing but misguided and embarrassing drivel from beginning to end and that it will probably mark the end of your career if anyone actually gets to read it. This is an annoying neurosis to be subjected to, but for my part I find that if I've become involved enough with the story to give it my best shot, I'm seemingly bound to worry obsessively about it until I actually see it on the rack in Forbidden Planet and realize that it's in the lap of the gods and that further anxiety is futile.

Reading back through this overlengthy meander I have a sense of wandering all over the place, including a few tangents and the failure to explain things as clearly as I would have liked. This is because the field of writing is so large and complex an endeavor, like any job that you throw yourself into completely, and even a long-winded discourse like this can only begin to scratch the surface of it. There are things that I've left out and things that I've skipped over with too little explanation, but I hope that in the final analysis there will be at least something that aspiring writers are able to use. If not, I hope that the disjointed and disconnected tone of the piece will serve as a grim warning by demonstrating just what this bizarre and obsessive profession eventually does to your brain. The timid need venture no farther. For the rest, I hope this sketchy preliminary map will at least allow them to avoid the worst of the snake pits and patches of quicksand, and find a career as emotionally and intellectually rewarding as the one which I'm enjoying at present. Good luck.

—ALAN MOORE

AFTERWORDS

Hmm. Well, having just read the foregoing piece for the first time in maybe fifteen years, I'd have to say it's not that bad. Conceivably, for someone starting as a writer in the field, the piece provides good basic methods of approach that were appropriate to the comics landscape of their day; that are probably at least harmless even if adopted in today's much-altered industry, much-altered world. It is still both desirable and necessary to consider all the elements explored within the essay...theme, location, pacing, character and so forth...even if the story one writes is intended for some newly-minted media or marketplace. The only caveat I'd level at the piece is that it was composed in simpler, far less complex times, and by a simpler, far less complex individual: someone a few years into his career attempting to describe the various processes of his craft as honestly and lucidly as he was capable of doing at the time. Someone who, whilst he may have accurately predicted that the future of the medium would be a furious and incessant state of constant change, had no idea just what those changes would mean for him personally or for the comic field in general.

Writing For Comics, while it may still have some utility for persons starting in the field, is next to useless from the viewpoint of someone who's worked within the field for fifteen, twenty, twenty-five years. Somebody for whom the problem is no longer how one starts upon a story or commences a career, but rather how one meaningfully continues as a writer after all those early, then-unreachable goals have been accomplished. When all the preceding instructions on pacing and structure and character have been absorbed so completely into one's daily practice and have become as natural and instinctive as the drawing of one's breath, what then? What's next? Where do you go when the perfecting and the polishing of all these literary skills is over, done with, finished to the best of your abilities? How do you keep at bay a fatal boredom with your own lame, over-used techniques, your tedious and unvarying style? The roadmap into comic scripting that *Writing For Comics* does its utmost to provide the reader with only extends so far and begs the question of what happens if you ever find that you've run our of road.

Consider these brief end-notes, then, as a rough and incomplete list of tenets and axioms that might be of use to someone who finds themselves a decade or so further down the path of writing than the reader that *Writing For Comics* was originally aimed at. An advanced class for those few remaining students whose lives weren't completely ruined by the first course of instruction. *X-Treme Writing for Comics.*

One of the first things to consider is style. The conventional wisdom everywhere within the fields of commercial art suggests that it is wisest to develop an easily-recognized style, a look or a feel that will instantly bring your name to mind for the audience. Now, even a cursory glance at the highest-earning cartoonists or writers or musicians will seemingly support this theory: the top-of-their-field authors who've essentially been writing the same book over and over again for the duration of their highly lucrative careers. The popular newspaper strip that's been recycling the same characters and gags for decades. The fifth platinum-selling album that's exactly the same as the first platinum-selling album. If your ambition is to become a rich person, then the above strategy clearly makes sense: find your golden rut and stick to it. Dig it deeper. If on the other hand

your ambition is to be a writer, a creator, then know that creativity is an ongoing and progressive phenomenon and that stasis and stagnation is sure death to it. If you wish to be a creator, then be assured that the actual problem lies in **avoiding** an easily recognized style. This is actually much trickier than its sounds, and requires diligence, although there are (largely contra-intuitive) ways of shortening the odds in your favor.

One excellent, if brutal and expensive, way of keeping a style fresh is to keep an eye on the devices and approaches that you are using. If you can even detect or notice a particular trick then this almost certainly means that you have done it more than once, and that it is thus in danger of becoming "part of your style", to put it charitably, or, more accurately, of becoming a cliché. Get rid of it. All that stuff I said a few chapters back about changing scenes with clever panel-to-panel linkages? Forget it. It was becoming a cliché even as I was writing those words, a technique that I pretty much abandoned straight after *Watchmen.* The captions filled with thoughtful, image-laden prose that initially drew so much attention to my work and which for a while I assumed to be the commercial backbone of my writing abilities? Dead in the water after those last issues of *Swamp Thing* and *Miracleman;* extravagant verbal showing-off that was fine for its time but in danger of becoming a joke if incessantly repeated. Just because you **can** do a particular thing well doesn't mean that you **have** to do it incessantly. Quite the reverse: be more original in your effects and use them more sparingly. That way they will be more of a surprise, will be more powerful and will thus go a lot further.

Of course, it isn't just the repetition of stylistic devices that one must vigilantly guard against, but also against repetition in more rarefied story elements such as tone and content. If your stories are receiving praise for their somber, thoughtful tone then that is precisely the time at which you should consider doing something lightweight and stupid. If your terse crime-dramas are earning you acclaim then maybe you should try writing comedy, or historical documentary or a dumb superhero comic. As D.H. Lawrence once advised, we should immerse ourselves in the least desirable element, and then swim. If there is some genre or form of subject matter that you have always avoided, it may be that it is there you will encounter the challenges and revelations that will advance you as a writer. Or, as one of Brian Eno's *Oblique Strategies* cards helpfully asks "What **wouldn't** you do?"

If we can discover and identity our limitations as writers then we have an opportunity for a kind of ju-jitsu dynamic where we can work off of those limitations to actually further ourselves. That is not to say that this is easy. Rather, it is easy's exact opposite, since from this perspective "easy" is what gets us into trouble in the first place. Easy creative decisions, easy thinking, approaches that will make the demands of writing for a living easier to bear: all these things can be fatal to the creative instinct, or at very least, less than fully nourishing. Make things hard for yourself. Attempt things that you are not sure that you can accomplish: if you're certain that you can do a thing, this means that there is little to no point in actually doing it. The reason you're

sure you can do it is that you or someone else has done it already. This work will teach you and your readers precisely nothing.

It is much more exciting and thus creatively energizing if you are attempting something where you are uncertain of its outcome, where you don't know if it will work or not. And this is only the beginning. Eventually, increasingly confident of your talents to make a workable story out of most anything, you will come to regard being merely unsure of a work's outcome as far too facile an approach. Instead, you may graduate to only attempting works which you privately suspect to be impossible. This is no bad thing, and if rigorously applied would weed out a great many dull and repetitive creators from the world while at the same time increasing the world's relatively meager cache of genuine unexpected marvels.

Work without a safety net. Ignore

everything I said in this essay's opening chapters about thinking through your plot and structure and characterization before embarking on the story. When you are a writer of some experience and prowess, it should be well within your capabilities to simply launch yourself at the deep end with a good opening idea and then trust your own mysterious processes to let plot and structure and nuances of character emerge from the narrative as you go along. This is how all of the comics in the *America's Best* line have been written, from the most innocuous *Tom Strong* light adventure romp, to the *Greyshirt* episode with four different time-frames on four different stories of an apartment building, to *Promethea* #12 with a structure so intricate and unlikely that I'm still not entirely sure how we accomplished it.

Apparent recklessness is actually an approach with multiple beneficial applications. In terms of crafting your stories, it will lend them an energy and unpredictability inaccessible by other means. In terms of managing your overall career, recklessness can also be very useful in avoiding some of more insidious and difficult-to-spot traps and snares which may be waiting for your talent down the road. The trap of reputation, for example. In this scenario, having garnered a considerable reputation or level of acclaim, one becomes paralyzed by the dreadful thought of losing it all by doing something...undignified. Uncool. This is a trap. Reputation is a trap that will turn you into a lifeless marble bust of yourself before you're even dead. And then of course there is Reputation's immortal big brother, Posterity, worrying about which has driven better women and men than you into the asylum. All these

things...reputation, posterity, cool...should be tested to destruction by a course of deliberate sabotage. As the often-illuminating *Escape* and *New Musical Express* cartoonist Shaky Kane once remarked, "Don't be cool. Like everything." If you find yourself in danger of being taken seriously, then try to do something which undermines or sabotages that perception in some way. If your talent is of any genuine worth, it should be able to weather squalls of unpopularity and audience incomprehension. The only thing that might seriously endanger either your talent or your relationship with your talent is if you suddenly found yourself fashionable.

Take risks. Fear nothing, especially failure. As a living and progressive process, your writing should constantly be looking for the next high windswept precipice to throw itself over. And if your first glimpse of the drop beneath you turns your stomach with its immensity, then so much the better. The higher the drop, the longer you have to...I don't know. Knit a helicopter or something...before you hit bottom.

As for posterity, don't drive yourself mad worrying about that shit. It isn't up to you. And anyway, when the Universe ends in ten billion years time it really isn't going be that important who was famous for how long. Take the long view. William Blake held only one exhibition during his lifetime, receiving only one review which concluded that he was "an unfortunate lunatic". Or there's that beautiful two-page long story by Lord Dunsany in which an artist struggles long and hard to win the attentions of Fame, only to see Fame parading herself around town on the arm of lesser talents, men less deserving than he of her attentions. Finally, after she has passed him in the street without a second glance one time too many, the artist can bear it no more and calls out after her, asking why she never gives him a second look when he has worked hard all his life to win her attentions. Fame looks back at him and smiles. "I'll see you in fifty years, in the pauper's graveyard behind the workhouse."

With regard to how you think about your work, avoid at all cost coming to conclusions. A conclusion is an ending. If your writing is still alive and vital, then it is because you are still asking difficult questions about yourself and your work and the relation between the two. The question I cited some chapters back, "Where do you get your ideas from?", is still fifteen years later a major source of fascination and impetus in my working and personal lives. Don't be afraid of considering peculiar or even entirely alien ideas, and if all they do is throw up a thousand new insoluble questions then so much the better. Questions are an energy that will fuel your writing, even if...especially if...you are never able to answer them to your own satisfaction. Entertaining hordes of questions will maintain the forward momentum of your mind, your work and your life. Don't worry about going too far. There isn't a Too Far. And if there is, it's absolutely **the** place to be seen.

Finally, if you want to be a truly great writer, it is perhaps worth remembering that even in this, it is more important to be a good human being than it is to be a good writer. The artists...writers, painters, musicians...whose voices speak loudest to us across the centuries are those that turned out to have the most profound souls, those who turned out to actually have something to say that was of lasting human value. Love people. Love yourself and love the world. It's only when we love things that we really, truly see them in their most lucid and perfect aspect; that we truly know them. And if you want to write about something, then you must know it, must understand it as fully as possible. Must love it, even if it is unlovable. Particularly if it is unlovable. Hey, now you're a professional writer, why not volunteer to give a talk to a group of murderers and rapists over at the nearest prison? How could anyone fail to benefit in understanding from an experience like that? What could be damaged except maybe prejudices and preconceptions? Immerse yourself in the least desirable element and swim.

Okay, that's about it. The basic message is "Ignore everything I said in the previous section of the book. I was young, confused, and nowhere near old or mad enough." Just be advised that I'll probably be writing a postscript to this essay around 2020 that will say just the same things about the advice I'm dishing out to you here.

Beyond that, you're on your own, pal.

Alan Moore
Northampton
May 16th, 2003.

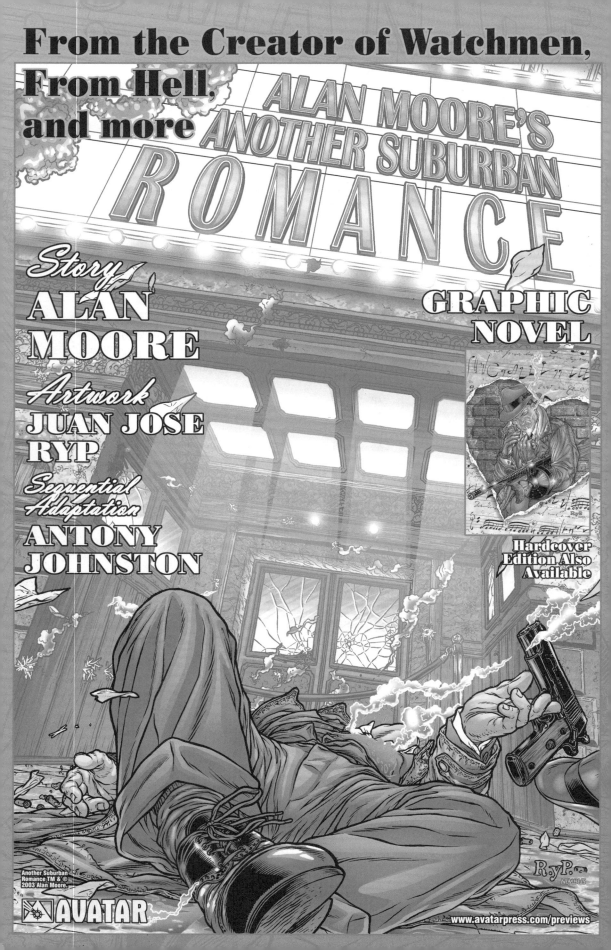